Our Bodies

Written by Kerrie Shanahan

Series Consultant: Linda Hoyt

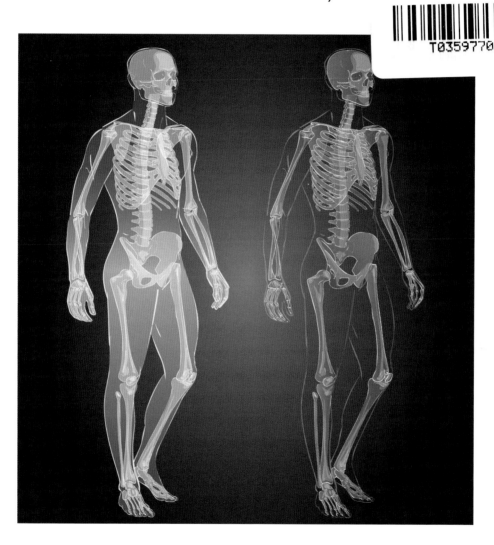

WorldWise
Content-based Learning

Contents

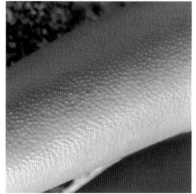
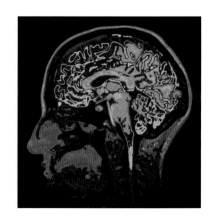

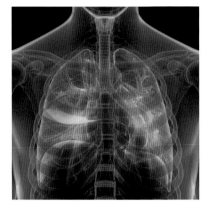

Introduction

Are you ready to be amazed?
Well get ready … now!

As you explore what goes on inside your body, you will find out some incredible facts about the remarkable **organs** and systems that allow you to live.

- Your lungs and heart are supplying your body with the **oxygen** and other **nutrients** your body needs to live.

- Your body is turning the food you eat into the **energy** it needs to work.

- Your bones, **muscles**, skin, eyes, teeth and all the other parts of your body are doing unique and important jobs.

- Your brain is in charge of everything.

Possibly the most amazing part is that these very complex things happen without you even thinking about them.

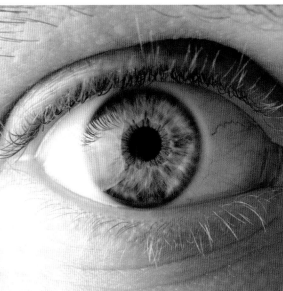

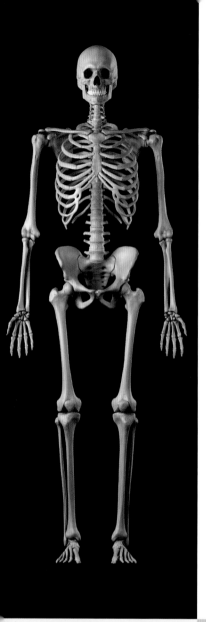

Chapter 1

From the inside out

The frame

Look at your body. What can you see?

Under your skin you have a **skeleton** that gives your body a structure and protects **organs** like your heart, lungs and brain. Your skeleton is strong and it enables you to move.

The skeleton is made up of hard bones that are connected by **joints**, which allow you to bend. The ends of each bone are covered in **cartilage**, which is like a cushion. Cartilage protects the ends of your bones from rubbing against each other at the joint.

Bones are made up of living **cells**, the tiny building blocks that join together to make up your body. New bone cells replace old ones all the time, even after you stop growing.

 Did you know?

Your skeleton is inside your body, but some animals, like crabs, have their skeletons on the outside. These skeletons are called exoskeletons.

The skeleton

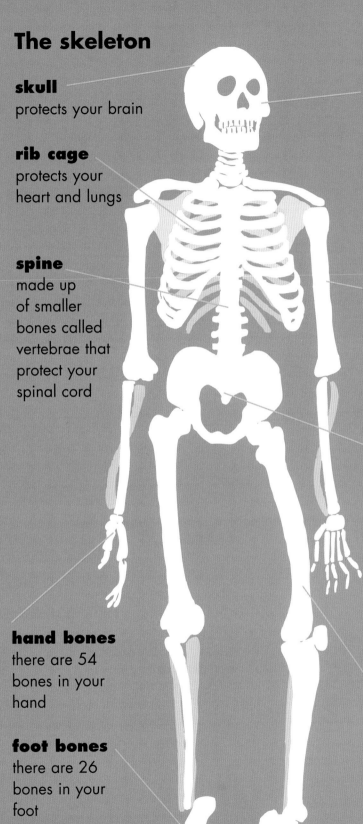

skull
protects your brain

face bones
protect your eyes,
ears and nasal
passages

rib cage
protects your
heart and lungs

spine
made up
of smaller
bones called
vertebrae that
protect your
spinal cord

**upper
arm bone
(humerus)**
joins your
shoulder to your
elbow

pelvis
supports your
spine

hand bones
there are 54
bones in your
hand

foot bones
there are 26
bones in your
foot

**thigh bone
(femur)**
joins your pelvis
to your knee

The movers

You use **muscles** to move your skeleton. Muscles are strong and stretchy and most muscles are attached to your bones by tough cords called **tendons**. You can move these muscles when you want to, such as when you want to walk or jump. You can control them.

Other muscles in your body have specific jobs. These muscles are found in organs like the heart and intestines. These muscles move automatically – you can't stop them from moving.

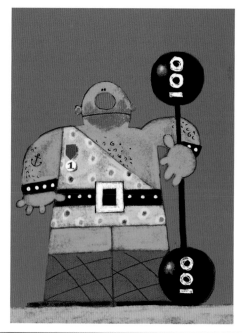

How do muscles work?

All muscles work by contracting and relaxing. Muscles often work in pairs to make your body move. One muscle contracts (shortens) as the other relaxes (gets longer). For example, when you move your arm up, the bicep contracts and becomes shorter. The tricep relaxes and becomes longer.

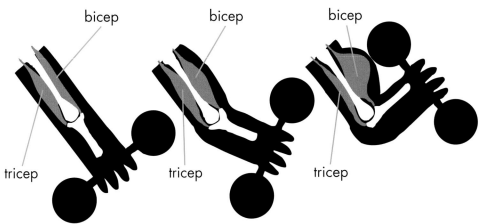

bicep   bicep   bicep

tricep   tricep   tricep

Muscle magic

How many muscles do you have?
Your body has more than 600 muscles.

Do you use more muscles to smile or frown?
It takes about 15 muscles to smile and about 45 muscles to frown.

Where is your biggest muscle?
It is in your bottom. It is called the *gluteus maximus*.

Where is your smallest muscle?
It is in your ear. It is called the *stapedius*.

How much do muscles weigh?
Muscles weigh about 40 per cent of your body's weight.

Which muscle is the most flexible?
Your tongue is your most flexible muscle!

Chapter 2

Skin, hair, nails and teeth

Skin

Skin protects the inside of your body from damage and disease. It helps to keep your body at the right temperature.

Your skin is made up of three layers. The top layer is called the epidermis. This is where old skin **cells** are continually falling off and being replaced by new skin cells. The second layer is called the dermis. Nerve cells, sweat glands and blood vessels are found in the dermis. The third layer is a layer of fat, which helps to keep you warm.

Skin stuff!

An adult's skin weighs about three to four kilograms.

If you spread out your skin, it would measure around 1.8 square metres, about the size of the quilt on your bed.

Most of the dust in your house is made up of dead skin cells.

You grow a new skin every two weeks.

A person loses 18 kilograms of skin in an average lifetime.

Your skin allows you to feel things. It contains tiny nerve endings that can sense pain, heat, cold and the faintest touches. These nerve endings send messages to your brain. When it receives a message, your brain decides what to do and then sends a message back to the part of the body that needs to react.

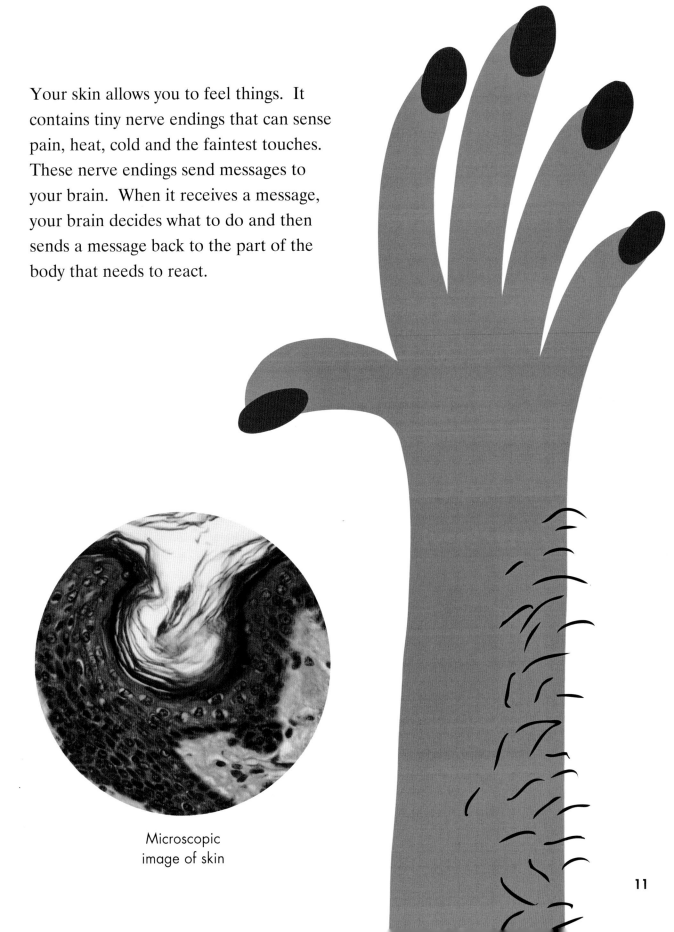

Microscopic
image of skin

Hair

Most of your skin has hair on it. Hair helps the skin to stay at the right temperature. When it is cold, your hairs stand upright to trap the warm air next to your skin. When it is hot, your hairs lie flat so heat isn't trapped.

There are about 100,000 hairs on a human head.

Nails

Nails cover the tips of your fingers and toes. Nails are made of layers of a protein called **keratin**, which is the same substance in skin and hair. The hard surface of your nails protects the sensitive skin underneath. If you injure your fingernail or toenail, it will bruise and may fall off. A new nail will grow in its place.

Did you know?

Your fingernails grow faster than your toenails.

? Did you know?

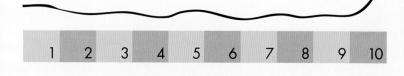

1	2	3	4	5	6	7	8	9	10

How fast does the hair on your head grow?
It can grow up to 10 centimetres a year.

How fast do nails grow?
They can grow up to five millimetres a month. A woman once grew her fingernails six metres long.

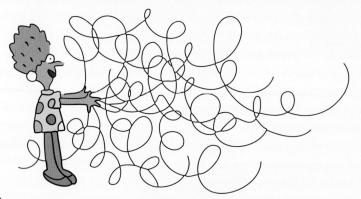

Teeth

Humans have two sets of teeth in their life. Scientists think this is because a baby's jaw is too small to hold a full set of adult teeth. Children have a set of smaller teeth that fall out and are replaced with the second set of teeth as the jaw gets bigger.

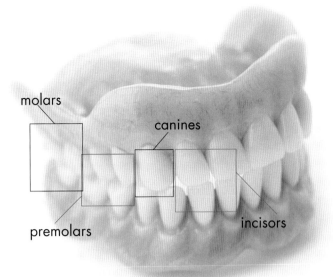

molars

canines

premolars

incisors

Teeth care hints

- Brush and floss your teeth.
- Drink water.
- Avoid sugary foods and drinks.
- Visit a dentist.

Teeth talk

Incisors cut and chop food.

Canines tear food.

Premolars crush and grind food.

Molars work with your tongue to help you swallow food.

? Did you know?

- When a dog chews on a bone, it is cleaning its teeth. This helps keep a dog's teeth strong and healthy.

- Sharks grow new teeth all the time. If they lose a tooth, a new one grows straight away. A shark can lose and regrow about 2,000 teeth in a year!

Chapter 3
The control centre

Think about a time when you learned something new. Maybe it was riding a bike, playing a new video game or solving a maths problem. How do you think you learned to do these things? Well, it's probably no surprise that your brain made it possible. In fact, your brain makes everything you do possible. It controls all the things your body does!

Brain facts

An adult brain weighs nearly 1.5 kilograms.

The brain fills the top half of the head.

The brain is faster and more powerful than any computer.

The left side of your brain controls the right side of your body, and the right side of your brain controls the left side of your body.

Brain basics

The brain is a grey, spongy, wrinkly **organ**. It is situated inside your head, protected by your skull. It is the control centre of your whole body.

The brain is made up of different parts. Each part is responsible for different things within your body. All the parts work together to make your body and all its systems run smoothly.

Your brain keeps your body working. It allows your **muscles** to move. It lets you remember both recent and long-ago events. Your brain tells you to sweat if you are hot and shiver when you are cold. It even lets you know when to feel happy or sad.

Parts of the brain

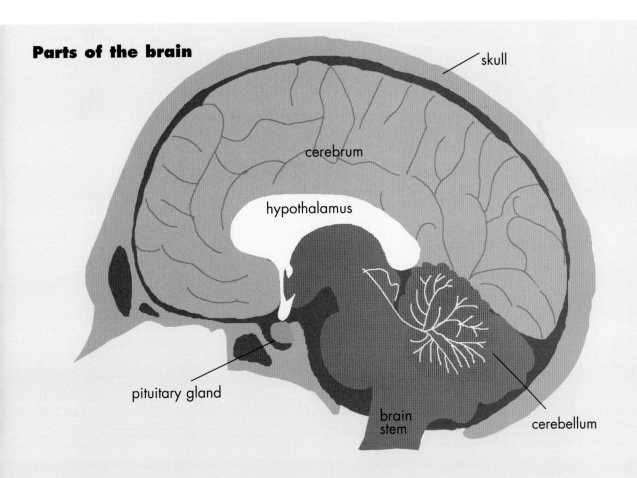

skull

cerebrum

hypothalamus

pituitary gland

brain stem

cerebellum

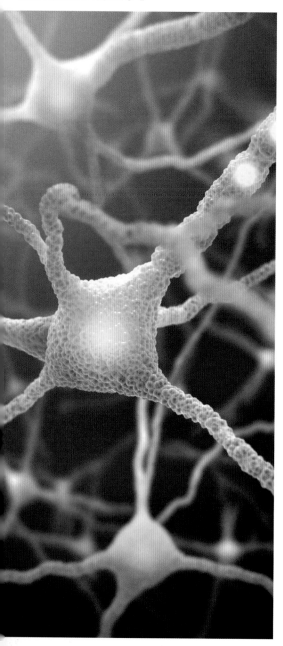

Getting the message through

We know the brain is responsible for controlling everything we do. But, how does it do this?

Your brain controls everything you do by sending and receiving messages to and from all parts of the body. The brain receives information about what is happening inside you and around you. It works out what the information means and then sends messages to tell your body how to react. These messages travel to and from the brain through the **nervous system**.

The nervous system is a pathway of nerves that runs throughout your body. Each nerve is made up of billions of tiny nerve **cells**. Information is passed from one nerve cell to another through chemicals that trigger an electrical impulse. This electrical impulse moves from one nerve cell to the next. This continues until the message gets through.

And all of this happens instantly – at lightning-quick speed!

Nimble nerves

Each message from the brain travels at more than 400 kilometres per hour.

There are about one billion nerve neurons (nerve cells) in your brain.

Your nervous system is always working – even when you're asleep.

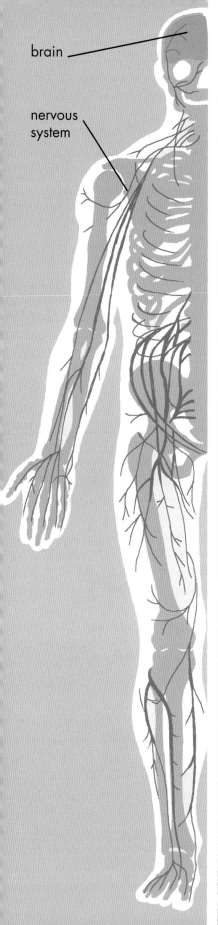

brain

nervous system

Bang!

The starter gun goes off. The sprinter springs out of her blocks. She pumps her arms and propels her legs forwards. Her nervous system is working hard! Messages are being sent continually to and from her brain. Messages are sent to her brain from her ears. *Start running!* Messages are sent to her muscles to move. *Fast!* Her brain sends messages to her heart and lungs. *Work harder!* The brain controls all parts of her body as she sprints to the finish line.

Chapter 4

Eye see!

One of the most important senses we have is our sight. Our eyes, brain and **nervous system** work together so that we can see.

How does the eye work?

Light enters your eye through the **pupil**. It hits the **lens**, and the lens focuses the light upside down on the **retina**. This upside-down image is converted into nerve signals. The **optic nerve** passes these signals on to the brain.

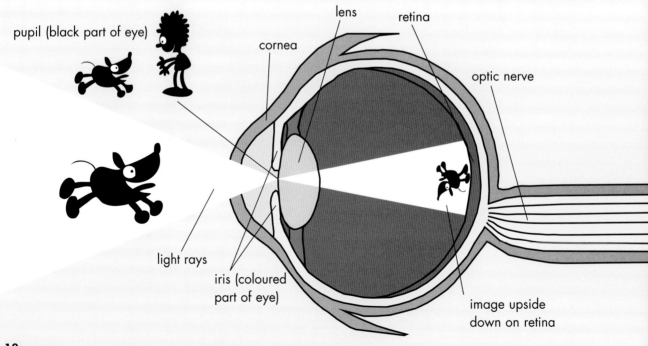

pupil (black part of eye)

cornea

lens

retina

optic nerve

light rays

iris (coloured part of eye)

image upside down on retina

What do tears do?

Tears keep your eyes moist. Every time you blink, tears wash your eyes. Tears also help to kill bacteria, which protects eyes from infection.

Why do eyelids blink?

As well as helping to keep the eyes moist, you blink automatically when something gets too close to your eye, when a bright light comes on, or when a speck of dust gets into your eye. Blinking protects your eyes. **Muscles** in your eyelids can make you blink up to five times per second.

What do eyelashes do?

Eyelashes help to protect your eyes from dust and insects. They grow on the edge of your eyelids.

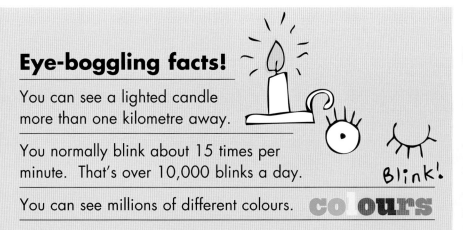

Eye-boggling facts!

You can see a lighted candle more than one kilometre away.

You normally blink about 15 times per minute. That's over 10,000 blinks a day.

You can see millions of different colours.

Blink!

colours

Thinking like a scientist

Look at your eye in the mirror. What parts can you identify? Can you see your pupil? Sometimes it changes size. Why might this happen?

Chapter 5

Your lungs and heart

The ins and outs of breathing

When you breathe in, or inhale, air enters your body through your nostrils and your mouth. The air we inhale is made up of a gas called **oxygen**. Your body needs oxygen to survive. Oxygen provides **energy** to the millions of **cells** throughout your body.

After you inhale, the oxygen travels down your **trachea** (also known as the windpipe) and enters your lungs. Lungs are soft, pink **organs** found underneath your ribs.

You have two lungs that expand when they fill with air. The oxygen that fills your lungs travels through tiny pathways and eventually disperses into your bloodstream. This oxygen is then carried by red blood cells to all parts of the body.

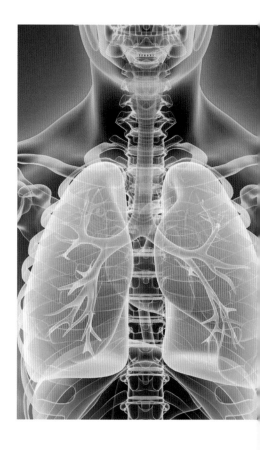

Try this!

Place your hands on your chest and take a deep, slow breath in through your nose. Now slowly release the air by breathing out through your mouth. Did you feel your chest rise and fall?

After breathing in, what is the next thing you must do? Breathe out! When you breathe out, or exhale, your body is getting rid of the old air that it no longer needs. This air is made up of a gas called carbon dioxide.

The **respiratory system** is the name given to the system in your body that allows you to breathe in oxygen-rich air and breathe out stale air. The lungs are the main organs in the respiratory system.

Your beating heart

Your heart is always beating. Twenty-four hours a day, seven days a week, all year round – year after year, after year. Your beating heart keeps you alive. Its role is to pump blood around your body. And this is vital because blood carries oxygen and **nutrients** to all cells in your body.

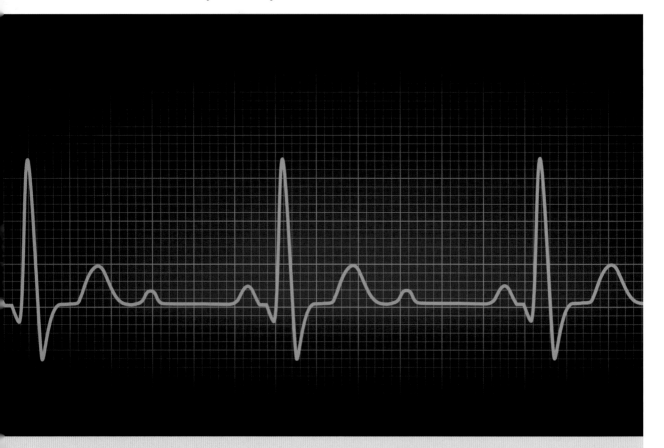

Heart facts

Your heart beats 60 to 100 times per minute.
That's more than 30 million beats a year!

Your heart pumps about 43,000 litres of blood
each day. That's enough to fill 150 baths!

Your heart is about the size of your clenched fist.

Put your index and middle finger under your jawline or on your wrist. What do you feel?

You will feel a beat. This beating is the blood being pumped through your body by your heart.

Count how many times you feel the beat in a minute. This is called your heart rate or your pulse.

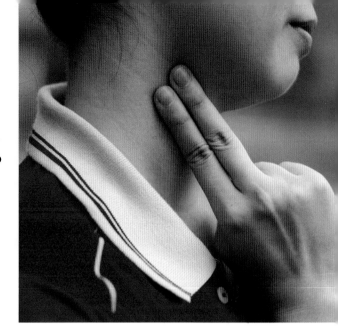

Heart parts

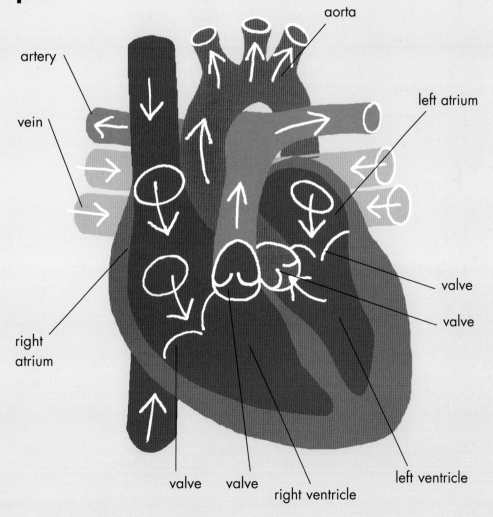

aorta

artery

vein

left atrium

valve

valve

right atrium

valve

valve

right ventricle

left ventricle

What is blood?

Blood is the red liquid that is pumped around your body by your heart. Your blood is constantly circulating … and quickly. In fact, it takes only about a minute for blood to reach all the cells in your body.

Blood, along with the heart, is part of the circulatory system. This system allows all cells to receive oxygen and nutrients. It also takes away waste products, such as carbon dioxide, from the cells.

What is blood made of?

- Red blood cells, which carry oxygen.
- White blood cells, which fight disease.
- Plasma, which is a yellowish liquid that carries the other cells.
- Platelets, which help stop bleeding if you are cut.

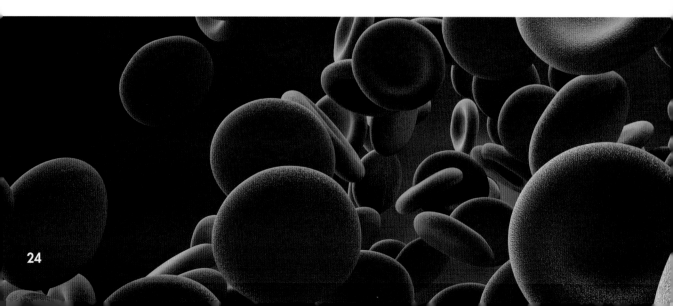

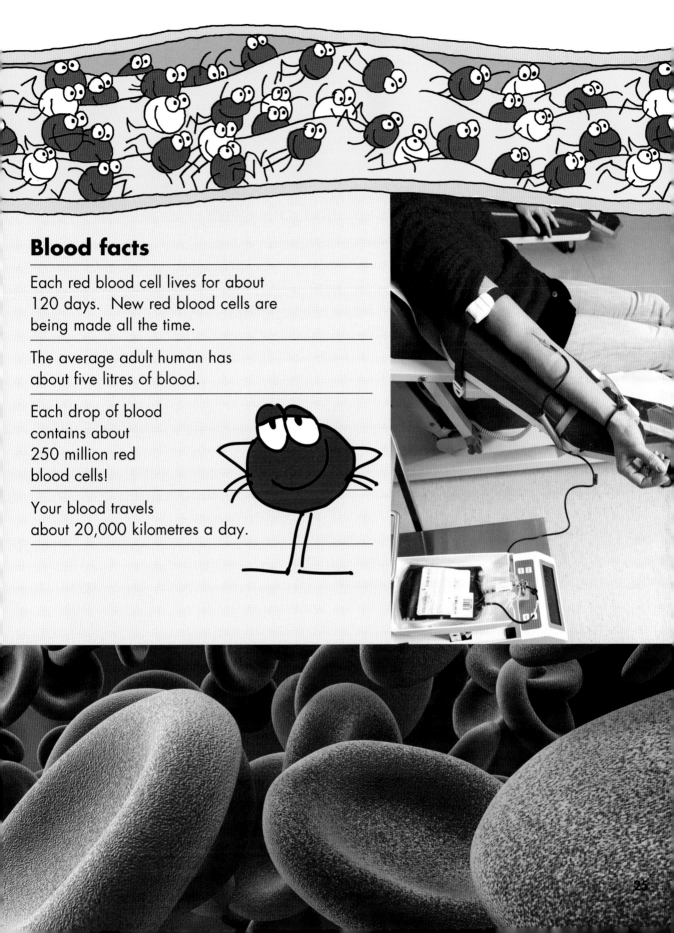

Blood facts

Each red blood cell lives for about 120 days. New red blood cells are being made all the time.

The average adult human has about five litres of blood.

Each drop of blood contains about 250 million red blood cells!

Your blood travels about 20,000 kilometres a day.

What does a red blood cell do?

Your body is made up of about 50 trillion cells. There are many different types of cells and each type has a special job to do in your body.

Red blood cells have the specialised role of transporting oxygen throughout the body and taking waste (carbon dioxide) to the lungs.

Hi, I'm a red blood cell.

I am so small you can only see me under a very powerful microscope. Along with trillions of other red blood cells, I make up blood.

Every cell in your body needs oxygen to work properly. I provide these cells with the oxygen they need. Your heart, the engine of the body, pumps me around your body through tubes called **arteries** and **veins**.

This is us under a microscope.

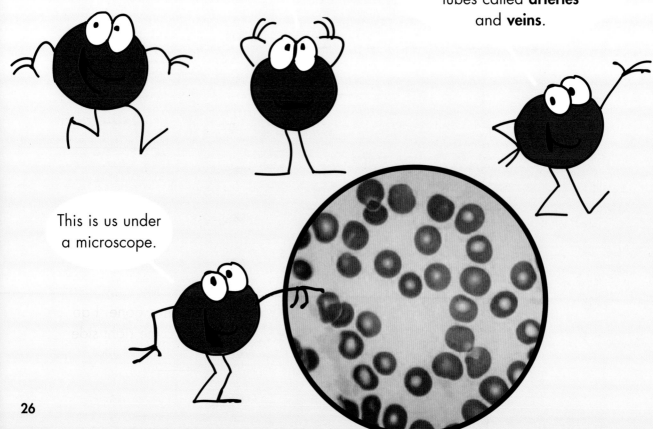

Respiratory and circulatory system

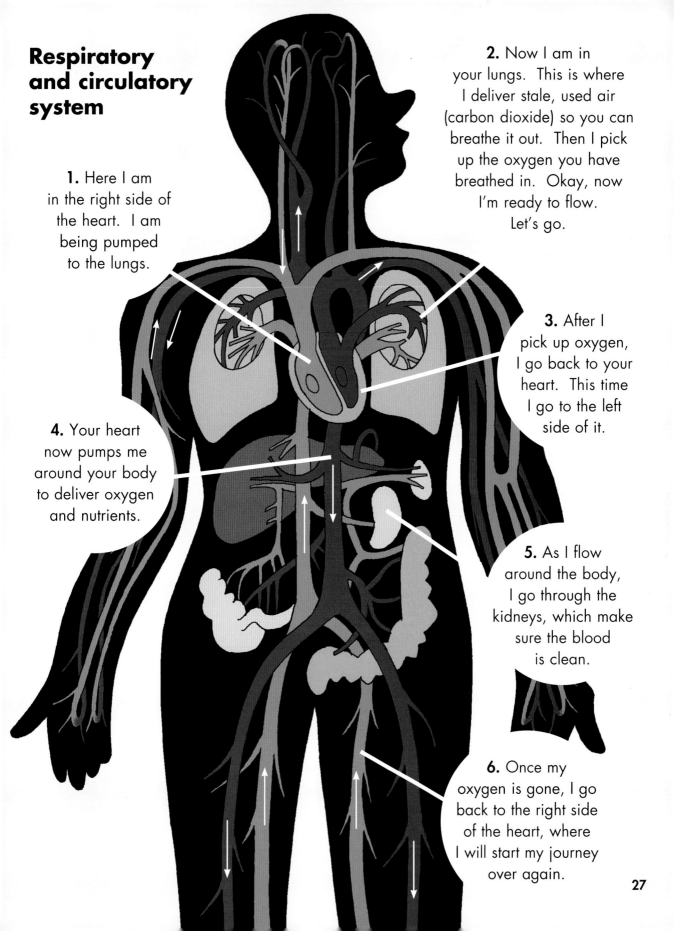

1. Here I am in the right side of the heart. I am being pumped to the lungs.

2. Now I am in your lungs. This is where I deliver stale, used air (carbon dioxide) so you can breathe it out. Then I pick up the oxygen you have breathed in. Okay, now I'm ready to flow. Let's go.

3. After I pick up oxygen, I go back to your heart. This time I go to the left side of it.

4. Your heart now pumps me around your body to deliver oxygen and nutrients.

5. As I flow around the body, I go through the kidneys, which make sure the blood is clean.

6. Once my oxygen is gone, I go back to the right side of the heart, where I will start my journey over again.

Chapter 6

The digestive system

Food is the fuel for your body. It gives you **energy**. Food also provides your body with **nutrients**. Nutrients allow your body to grow, repair itself and fight disease. But how does the food you eat do these vital things?

The **digestive system** turns food into fuel for your body. It breaks down food into tiny particles that are eventually absorbed by the body. It also gets rid of waste that the body doesn't need.

Feeling hungry?

The process of breaking down food so your body can use it is called digestion. Digestion begins before you even start eating. When you smell food, **saliva** forms in your mouth, and as you eat, the saliva begins to soften the food.

As you eat, your teeth and tongue break down the food into pieces that are small enough for you to swallow. Your teeth play an important role in this first stage of digestion. Different types of teeth have different roles in breaking down food.

Did you know?

Saliva glands produce over one litre of saliva each day!

Breaking it down

When food is small enough to swallow, it goes down your throat (or esophagus) and into your stomach. Your stomach is like a mixer. It moves the food around and around using strong **muscles**. Inside your stomach there is liquid called **gastric juice**. This liquid helps to break down the food that is being mixed around in your stomach. Gastric juices also kill some germs that you may have swallowed.

From the stomach, the tiny food particles enter the small intestine. It is here that these particles are broken down further into nutrients that can be absorbed into the blood. Smaller **organs** called the liver, the gallbladder and the pancreas help the small intestine with this job.

The food particles that are left over go to the large intestine where water is absorbed from them. The leftover waste is pushed out of the body.

The food you eat has stored energy inside it. When your body breaks this food down, the energy can be used. Your body needs this energy. It uses energy all the time.

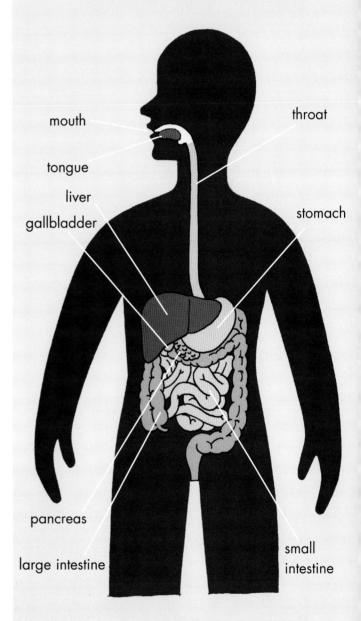

The digestive system

mouth

tongue

liver

gallbladder

throat

stomach

pancreas

large intestine

small intestine

Conclusion

Your body in summary

Body system	Main parts	Purpose
Skeletal	Bones, **cartilage**	To give the body a frame and to protect the insides of the body.
Muscular	**Muscles**, **tendons**	To allow the body to move.
Nervous	Brain, nerve cells	To receive and work out information sent to and from the senses.
Circulatory	Heart, blood, **arteries**, **veins**	To supply **cells** with **oxygen** and **nutrients** and to remove waste.
Respiratory	Lungs, **trachea**	To breathe in oxygen and breathe out stale air.
Digestive	Stomach, small intestine, large intestine	To turn food into **energy** and to remove waste.

Glossary

arteries the tubes that carry blood full of oxygen away from the heart

cartilage a flexible material on the end of bones to stop them from rubbing together

cells the tiny building blocks that join together to make your body

digestive system parts of the body used to digest food

energy fuel from food that keeps your body going

gastric juice liquid found in your stomach that breaks down food to digest it

joint a place in your body where your bones meet so you can bend and move

keratin the substance that makes up hair and nails

lens the part of your eye that focuses the image the eye sees

muscle strong, elastic tissue that helps you to move

nervous system the body's network of nerves that send messages to and from your brain

nutrients the parts of food that keep you strong and healthy

optic nerve the nerve that passes signals from the eyes to the brain

organ a part of your body with a special function, like the heart or brain

oxygen an important gas in the air that your lungs breathe in

pupil the part of your eye that lets light in so you can see

respiratory system parts of the body used for breathing

retina the cells in the eyes that receive the image you see

saliva the digestive juice in your mouth

skeleton the bones that give you shape and structure

tendon a cord of tough tissue that connects a muscle with a bone

trachea a long tube in your neck that carries air in and out of your lungs

veins the tubes that carry blood back to the heart after it has gone around the body

Index